A Time for change

Thoughts of a simple black man

By Brandon Cephas

Copyright © 2020 Brandon Cephas

All rights reserved.

ISBN-13: 9798652123185

Dedication

To all those who lost their lives to racism and police brutality.

Rest in Power.

Table of Contents

Acknowledgment

First of all, I would like to thank my creator for giving me the gift of word. Through this talent, I was able to create this poetry book **A time for Change** that I was really passionate about.

My next thank you goes to one of my biggest fans, Julianne Scott. She has been very supportive, giving feedback to help enhance my perspective and reviewing and fixing any little grammar mistakes in my projects.

I also would like to thank my friends and family, and to the reader of this book, my last poem is dedicated to you.

Little black boy

Hey! Little black boy!

Get over here!

Why are your hands held high?

Let me search you

Did you steal, do drugs? What crime are you trying to hide?

Get down, lay down - while I am trying to decide.

Oh, little black boy! Is all this squirming around trying to make me believe

That while I pin my knee into your neck,

Are you trying to say you can't breathe?

Foolish little black boy.

You spoke, so you are just fine.

But if I feel threatened, I will reach for my nine,

Click Clack

And turn your lights out in a drop of a dime.

Hey officer, what did I do wrong?
Were my pants sagging, was my hat turned back?
Was I too loud with my rap song?
What? Officer, why do I have to get down on my knees?
What? Lie down now? Sir, what are you doing?? I cannot breathe!
What did I do, what was my crime?
I can't feel it, I am losing it, and my oxygen is running out -
I think I'm out of time.

Hey officer, did you know you took that child of mine?
That little boy, with no prior offense, lost his life to crime.
What crime, you say? Well, the Hatred in your eyes.
He died because you refuse to act correctly and fairly in your job.
Now this red dot from afar, oh it's about to be real.
Bang
You are now dead as a doorknob.

Exhale

Or at least that's how I feel.

Lost

Broken, cold, scarred left alone

Changing the song to a different tone

Happiness left, joy is gone

I sing but to a different song

It's so clouded in here; there is no room for sight

To be in such darkness the absence of light

Without peace, judgment, wisdom, insight

I am lost to the world

In a world that isn't mine

I have forgotten what is precious

But I will find it back in due time.

White Silence

Like a piece of paper begging me not to write

Or dim flashlight in the darkness of night

You stand there while I am bleeding

But you don't see me, right?

You "don't see color," you only see black and white.

To you, my being is just an accessory to your life.

A tool bought at Target, a stool to increase your height

No wonder you get so angry when we burn things for what we think is right.

But when there is injustice, your jaws are shut tight.

Attitude

I got told about 99 problems

Yet I chose to drive slow

But with America slowly dying

I'm like, "how much more these people in power got to know?"

My brothers and sisters are getting executed!

I'm like, what's up with all this shit!?

You got people screaming f@%k the police!

And right now

I am really feeling it.

I'd like to believe it was written

Powerful words had me feeling like a king

But when I turn the television on, seeing how we are portrayed

I see a different thing.

Slave chains turned into minimum wages

And our castles that should be seating our kings and queens

Are sometimes buildings filled with cages

Or boarded-up houses, filled with roaches and laced with ripped screens.

I am frustrated.

And though I hear the cries for unity.

This racism culture got me aggravated.

And I feel my brothers and sisters are just lined up for the guillotines.

But I continue to pour my truth onto paper.

It seems I must if I want to be a change in the system.

To educate every gatekeeper.

Of this white privilege ecosystem

I'm ready

Justice

Justice for Floyd

That's just one more step for the goal I need

I need those cops to be accountable, who shot Breonna while she was asleep

I need that father-son duo who thought it was just fine

To shoot Ahmaud Arbery, regardless of what he was doing that time

I need to see Amy Cooper behind bars

Because her words had a murderous tone

If it wasn't for technology

Christian Cooper would have mental scars

Or worse yet

Died in that park alone.

So please miss me with that nonsense, telling me it's hard to convict

When if it was a person of color with no badge, hell, even with one

It would be fast as shit.

Because our skin tone comes with a guilty verdict.

I mean really, when are you going to take that blindfold off of Lady Justice?

Because clearly, she is still blind.

I am watching killers with badges go freely!

Yet you are telling me –

"Sir, it's still going to take some time."

A time for change

So much blood under the flag of "equality."

So many lies have been written

Hiding the hate crimes against you and me.

I ask

When will they see us?

Only when we scorch the land?

Do we need to start making examples?

To help them understand?

Or will the people in power stop worrying about being broke

And give back our lives, instead of writing us off as a joke.

And no, I am not talking about 40 acres.

No, not this time.

I am talking about being able to take a walk without being accused of a crime.

Being able to breathe instead of three cops on my spine.

Allowed to be curious without vigilante raising a shotgun in my face

Yet you want me to be compliant.

Telling me to wait?

When!?

When all my people are behind bars

So you can say that's when America is great.

Heh

Well, I tell you now people in power, that's not a good time to be late

Being late on promises will have us storming that gate

And no amount of police force you could call within the state

Can't stop a legion of protestors with their voices

As heavy as the Empire State

At the White House be damn sure

Their shouts and their cries will have penetrated

Until injustice is dead

And police brutality eradicated.

Somebody

Somebody

Somebody needs a hero

Somebody needs someone to care

Somebody out there hurting

Wishing you were there.

Somebody was left in the night

Somebody told someone else a lie

Somebody took a life

Somebody made you cry.

If we keep on living

With these hateful actions in our hearts

Know that all eyes will forever hold tears

And the world will be torn apart.

Teach yourself to love those that are different

Give your heart a chance to smile.

Let them know there is hope.

And very soon, the love which was only an inch will become a mile.

That one time...

He called me a liar.

"Hey, Son, got any weed on ya?"

No, sir, I do not smoke.

"What about that air freshener?"

I'm sorry, sir, was that a joke?

"I need you to be real with me, I am willing to let it slide."

...you want me to lie to you, trust in you as someone to confide… in?

Where do I begin? I was just stopped, and your lights flashed ever so brightly.

That, combined with your flashlight - my vision was ever so dim.

So when you rolled up on me, noticing my hands at 2 and 10

Telling me to relax

And I wonder

When?

When is it okay to relax this time?

When all I need to do is sneeze, and you can shout, your life was on the line.

Releasing several shots in me, and you get to go home feeling fine.

Come on man

You are just holding me here wasting my time

When you know my papers are legit

And yet you still are searching for a crime

What about how you flashed your lights, then turned them off,

So you could ride on up on my behind?

What if there was a deer in my sight at the time?

Causing me to stomp on my brakes, and having your car to crash into mine.

You see, I will never relax as long as you got that gun.

So you can say what you want and oh yea officer.

I am not your son.

Put your hands up!

"Put your hands up!"

Sir, how much higher can they be?

"You are resisting arrest."

I am not even moving!

"To tell you the truth, you got me feeling like you are going to attack."

"Hey! Stop reaching for my gun!"

Officer, my hands are behind my back.

"Make one more move, and I swear I will shoot you."

Sir, tell me what I've done!?

"We were told someone outside was looking suspicious."

Yeah, I was outside, but I wasn't the only one.

"I am so sick of this!"

Sir, sick of what I am not even trying to resist

Bang Bang Bang Bang Bang Bang!

"Why did you shoot him so many times?"

He looked like he was reaching for a weapon.

"Oh your life was on the line?"

Yup

"Really? I just checked his body, all he had was a phone."

Well, partner, you saw him, he was threatening by the actions he has shown

But don't worry about it. Partner, we are cops, and it's already known.

We will get away with it by calling it an accident.

Hell yeah, an accident! Let that be the tone!

So we can get a slap on a wrist and paid leave.

Killing two birds with one stone.

"Oh yeah, whew. It was a good thing my body cam was off."

I know mine too

So now this case will definitely be postponed.

My Pledge

My pledge

Is to live in a place, where I can be free

That's all I want to be - free.

I will do the hard work, I will do my time

As long as I have an equal opportunity at the finish line.

I will stand for justice and no, not just for color folk.

But for all humans, I will be one of the symbols of hope.

I will share love and give my shoulder for tears.

I will stand in front of hurt ones, protecting them from their fears.

I will breathe honesty and I will walk in truth

I will learn from the elderly and educate the youth.

So that when I die, there will be tears of joy

Knowing that I stood against every injustice

That my words gave praise and were not words that destroyed.

My Pledge

Perseverance

What is it?

It's climbing that mountain when it seems too tall

Taking wings into flight knowing one might fall

It's when you

Fight a thousand people with no way out

Swimming through a roaring river without the slightest of doubt

Knowing at all times to overcome and never stall

And with perseverance,

You will find it all.

Thank you

Thank you

Yes, I mean you.

You, who stood up

When no one asked you.

You, who still marched

Though tear gas swam in your eyes.

You, who protected a singled-out officer when everyone else only had violence in mind

You, who stopped the violence, when evil hid its intentions under the umbrella of being woke

You, who took a knee at the flag

You, who recorded all of it, while our brother was being choked.

You, who moves not just for the color of skin

But moves with so much love that every human deserves a win.

You, who does not back down

Using your words and stating you will fight

To free every soul from injustice no matter the plight.

You, who is and me who is you

With so much love and appreciation, I bow

And speak loudly with the voice I've been given!

Thank you.

Made in the USA
Middletown, DE
18 July 2020